HIGH C

SMOOTHIE RECIPES

for
WEIGHT GAIN

25 QUICK, EASY, HEALTHY AND NUTRITIOUS SMOOTHIE RECIPES TO HELP YOU GAIN HEALTHY WEIGHT

RACHELLE K. SANDERS

Copyright

Disclaimer

Disclaimer: The images in this book are for illustrative purposes only and may not perfectly replicate the end product based on individual variations in ingredients, techniques, and personal interpretation. Results may differ, but we hope the flavors remain delightful on your culinary journey.

Table of Contents

Peanut Butter Banana Bliss

Ingredients

- 1 Banana
- 2 tablespoons Peanut Butter
- 1 cup Whole Milk
- 1/2 cup Greek Yogurt
- 1 tablespoon Honey

Instructions

1. Peel and slice the banana.

2. In a blender, combine banana slices, peanut butter, whole milk, Greek yogurt, and honey.

3. Blend the ingredients until the mixture is smooth and creamy.

4. Taste the smoothie and adjust sweetness if necessary by adding more honey.

5. Pour the smoothie into a glass and enjoy the Peanut Butter Banana Bliss!

Note

- You can customize the thickness of the smoothie by adjusting the amount of milk or yogurt. Additionally, feel free to add a handful of ice cubes if you prefer a colder and more refreshing texture. This smoothie is not only delicious but also packed with energy from the combination of banana, peanut butter, and dairy. Enjoy!

Chocolate Avocado Delight

Ingredients

- 1 Avocado
- 2 scoops Chocolate Protein Powder
- 1 cup Almond Milk
- 1 tablespoon Chia Seeds

Instructions

1. Cut the avocado and remove the pit. Scoop out the flesh.

2. In a blender, combine the avocado, chocolate protein powder, almond milk, and chia seeds.

3. Blend the ingredients until the mixture is smooth and well combined.

4. Check the consistency, and if it's too thick, you can add more almond milk and blend again.

5. Pour the smoothie into a glass and, if desired, top it with a sprinkle of chia seeds for added texture.

6. Serve and savor the Chocolate Avocado Delight!

Note

- Adjust the sweetness by adding a touch of honey or another sweetener if desired. The combination of creamy avocado, rich chocolate protein powder, and the nutty flavor of almond milk creates a delicious and nutrient-packed smoothie. Enjoy this delightful and indulgent treat!

Mango Coconut Powerhouse

Ingredients

- 1 Mango
- 1/2 cup Coconut Milk
- 1/4 cup Oats
- 2 scoops Vanilla Protein Powder

Instructions

1. Peel and dice the mango.

2. In a blender, combine the diced mango, coconut milk, oats, and vanilla protein powder.

3. Blend the ingredients until you achieve a smooth and creamy consistency.

4. If the smoothie is too thick, you can add more coconut milk gradually until it reaches your desired thickness.

5. Pour the smoothie into a glass and, for added appeal, garnish it with a sprinkle of oats or coconut flakes.

6. Enjoy the Mango Coconut Powerhouse – a delicious and nutrient-packed smoothie!

Note

- Feel free to customize the sweetness by adjusting the amount of mango or adding a natural sweetener like honey. This smoothie combines the tropical flavors of mango and coconut with the energy boost from oats and protein powder, making it a perfect powerhouse drink. Enjoy the refreshing and nourishing goodness!

Berry Nut Explosion

Ingredients

- Mixed Berries (e.g., strawberries, blueberries, raspberries)
- 2 tablespoons Almond Butter
- 1 cup Whole Milk
- Handful of Spinach

Instructions

1. Wash the mixed berries thoroughly.

2. In a blender, combine the mixed berries, almond butter, whole milk, and a handful of spinach.

3. Blend the ingredients until the mixture is smooth and the spinach is well incorporated.

4. If the smoothie is too thick, you can adjust the consistency by adding more milk and blending again.

5. Pour the vibrant Berry Nut Explosion into a glass and enjoy the burst of flavors!

Note

- You can customize this smoothie by adding a natural sweetener like honey if you prefer a sweeter taste. The combination of antioxidant-rich berries, creamy almond butter, and the nutritional boost from spinach makes this smoothie both delicious and nutritious. Sip and savor the explosion of flavors!

Banana Nut Bread Smoothie

Ingredients

- 1 Banana
- Handful of Walnuts
- 1/4 cup Oats
- 1/2 teaspoon Cinnamon
- 1 cup Whole Milk

Instructions

1. Peel and slice the banana.
2. In a blender, combine banana slices, walnuts, oats, cinnamon, and whole milk.
3. Blend the ingredients until you achieve a smooth and creamy texture.
4. Taste the smoothie and adjust the sweetness or thickness by adding more banana or milk as needed.
5. Pour the Banana Nut Bread Smoothie into a glass, and if desired, sprinkle a dash of cinnamon on top.
6. Enjoy the delightful flavors reminiscent of banana nut bread in liquid form!

Note

- You can also add a touch of honey or maple syrup for additional sweetness. This smoothie brings together the comforting taste of banana nut bread with the goodness of walnuts and oats, making it a satisfying and nutritious treat. Cheers to a delicious and wholesome experience!

Avocado Almond Dream

Ingredients

- 1 Avocado
- 2 tablespoons Almond Butter
- 1/2 cup Greek Yogurt
- 1 tablespoon Honey
- 1 cup Almond Milk

Instructions

1. Cut the avocado, remove the pit, and scoop out the flesh.
2. In a blender, combine the avocado, almond butter, Greek yogurt, honey, and almond milk.
3. Blend the ingredients until you achieve a creamy and smooth consistency.
4. Taste the smoothie and adjust sweetness by adding more honey if desired.
5. If the smoothie is too thick, you can adjust the consistency by adding more almond milk.
6. Pour the Avocado Almond Dream into a glass, and optionally drizzle a bit of honey on top for decoration.
7. Enjoy the luscious and nutty goodness of the Avocado Almond Dream!

Note

- This smoothie is rich in healthy fats from avocado and almond butter, and the Greek yogurt adds a creamy texture. It's a delightful blend of flavors that makes for a satisfying and nutritious drink. Sip and savor the dreamy goodness!

Tropical Macadamia Madness

Ingredients

- 1 cup Pineapple chunks
- 1 cup Mango chunks
- 1/4 cup Macadamia Nuts
- 1/2 cup Coconut Milk

Instructions

1. Prepare the pineapple and mango by peeling and cutting them into chunks.

2. In a blender, combine the pineapple chunks, mango chunks, macadamia nuts, and coconut milk.

3. Blend the ingredients until you achieve a smooth and tropical-flavored consistency.

4. If you prefer a colder smoothie, you can add a handful of ice cubes and blend again.

5. Taste the smoothie and adjust sweetness or thickness by adding more fruits or coconut milk if needed.

6. Pour the Tropical Macadamia Madness into a glass, and garnish with a slice of pineapple or a sprinkle of shredded coconut if desired.

7. Enjoy the tropical paradise in a glass with the richness of macadamia nuts!

Note

- Macadamia nuts add a unique and buttery flavor to this tropical smoothie, making it a delightful and nutritious treat. Feel free to customize it based on your taste preferences. Cheers to the Tropical Macadamia Madness!

Cherry Almond Burst

Ingredients

- 1 cup Cherries (pitted)
- Handful of Almonds
- 2 scoops Vanilla Protein Powder
- 1 cup Almond Milk

Instructions

1. Pit the cherries if they aren't already pitted.
2. In a blender, combine the pitted cherries, almonds, vanilla protein powder, and almond milk.
3. Blend the ingredients until you achieve a smooth and luscious consistency.
4. If you prefer a colder smoothie, consider adding a few ice cubes before blending.
5. Taste the smoothie and adjust sweetness or thickness by adding more cherries or almond milk as needed.
6. Pour the Cherry Almond Burst into a glass, and optionally top it with a few whole almonds for added crunch.
7. Enjoy the burst of cherry flavor combined with the nutty goodness of almonds!

Note

- This smoothie is not only delicious but also packed with the goodness of cherries, almonds, and protein. Feel free to experiment with the ratio of cherries and almonds to suit your taste preferences. Sip and savor the Cherry Almond Burst!

Peach Cobbler Bliss

Ingredients

- 1 cup Peaches (sliced)
- 1/4 cup Oats
- 1/2 teaspoon Cinnamon
- 2 scoops Vanilla Protein Powder
- 1 cup Whole Milk

Instructions

1. Slice the peaches, ensuring they are ripe and sweet.

2. In a blender, combine the sliced peaches, oats, cinnamon, vanilla protein powder, and whole milk.

3. Blend the ingredients until you achieve a smooth and cobbler-like consistency.

4. If you prefer a thicker smoothie, you can add more oats gradually and blend again.

5. Taste the smoothie and adjust sweetness or spice by adding more peaches or cinnamon if desired.

6. Pour the Peach Cobbler Bliss into a glass, and optionally sprinkle a dash of cinnamon on top for a finishing touch.

7. Indulge in the delightful taste of a peach cobbler in liquid form!

Note

- This smoothie captures the essence of peach cobbler with the added benefits of oats and protein powder. Feel free to customize the recipe based on your preferences for sweetness and thickness. Enjoy the Peach Cobbler Bliss!

Strawberry Cheesecake Indulgence

Ingredients

- 1 cup Strawberries (hulled)
- 2 tablespoons Cream Cheese
- 1/2 cup Greek Yogurt
- 1 tablespoon Honey

Instructions

1. Hull the strawberries to remove the stems.
2. In a blender, combine the hulled strawberries, cream cheese, Greek yogurt, and honey.
3. Blend the ingredients until you achieve a smooth and creamy texture, resembling the richness of cheesecake.
4. Taste the smoothie and adjust sweetness by adding more honey if needed.
5. If you prefer a colder smoothie, you can add a handful of ice cubes and blend again.
6. Pour the Strawberry Cheesecake Indulgence into a glass, and optionally garnish with a strawberry slice on the rim.
7. Enjoy the luscious flavors of strawberry cheesecake in a refreshing and nutritious form!

Note

- This smoothie provides the delightful taste of strawberry cheesecake while incorporating the goodness of Greek yogurt. Customize the sweetness according to your preference and relish the indulgence of this delicious treat!

Blueberry Muffin Marvel

Ingredients

- 1 cup Blueberries
- 1/4 cup Oats
- 2 tablespoons Almond Butter
- 1 cup Almond Milk

Instructions

1. Rinse the blueberries thoroughly.
2. In a blender, combine the blueberries, oats, almond butter, and almond milk.
3. Blend the ingredients until you achieve a smooth and muffinlike consistency.
4. If you prefer a thicker smoothie, you can add more oats gradually and blend again.
5. Taste the smoothie and adjust sweetness by adding more blueberries or a natural sweetener if desired.
6. Pour the Blueberry Muffin Marvel into a glass, and optionally garnish with a few whole blueberries on top.
7. Enjoy the delightful taste reminiscent of a blueberry muffin!

Note

- This smoothie captures the essence of a blueberry muffin with the added benefits of oats and almond butter. Customize the sweetness and thickness to your liking, and savor the Blueberry Muffin Marvel!

Caramel Apple Crunch

Ingredients

- 1 Apple (peeled and sliced)
- 2 tablespoons Caramel Sauce
- 1/4 cup Oats
- 2 scoops Vanilla Protein Powder

Instructions

1. Peel and slice the apple, ensuring the core and seeds are removed.

2. In a blender, combine the sliced apple, caramel sauce, oats, and vanilla protein powder.

3. Blend the ingredients until you achieve a smooth and caramel-infused texture.

4. If you prefer a thicker smoothie, you can add more oats gradually and blend again.

5. Taste the smoothie and adjust sweetness by adding more caramel sauce or a natural sweetener if desired.

6. Pour the Caramel Apple Crunch into a glass, and optionally drizzle a bit of caramel sauce on top for extra indulgence.

7. Enjoy the delightful combination of caramel, apple, and oats in this tasty and satisfying smoothie!

Note

- This smoothie provides the flavors of a caramel apple with the added benefits of oats and protein powder. Customize the sweetness and thickness according to your preferences. Sip and savor the Caramel Apple Crunch!

Mocha Hazelnut Elixir

Ingredients

- 1 cup Coffee (cooled)
- 2 scoops Chocolate Protein Powder
- 1/4 cup Hazelnuts
- 1 cup Whole Milk

Instructions

1. Brew a cup of coffee and allow it to cool to room temperature.

2. In a blender, combine the cooled coffee, chocolate protein powder, hazelnuts, and whole milk.

3. Blend the ingredients until you achieve a smooth and mocha-infused texture.

4. If you prefer a colder smoothie, you can add a handful of ice cubes and blend again.

5. Taste the smoothie and adjust sweetness by adding more chocolate protein powder or a natural sweetener if desired.

6. Pour the Mocha Hazelnut Elixir into a glass, and optionally garnish with a sprinkle of crushed hazelnuts on top.

7. Enjoy the rich and energizing flavors of mocha and hazelnut in this delightful smoothie!

Note

- : Customize the sweetness and strength of coffee to suit your preferences. This smoothie combines the bold flavors of coffee with the richness of hazelnuts and chocolate protein powder for a satisfying treat. Sip and savor the Mocha Hazelnut Elixir!

Raspberry Pistachio Pleasure

Ingredients

- 1 cup Raspberries
- 1/4 cup Pistachios
- 1/2 cup Greek Yogurt
- 1 cup Almond Milk

Instructions

1. Rinse the raspberries thoroughly.
2. In a blender, combine the raspberries, pistachios, Greek yogurt, and almond milk.
3. Blend the ingredients until you achieve a smooth and vibrant consistency.
4. If you prefer a thicker smoothie, you can add more Greek yogurt gradually and blend again.
5. Taste the smoothie and adjust sweetness by adding more raspberries or a natural sweetener if desired.
6. Pour the Raspberry Pistachio Pleasure into a glass, and optionally garnish with a few crushed pistachios on top.
7. Enjoy the delightful combination of tart raspberries and the nutty flavor of pistachios in this refreshing smoothie!

Note

- Customize the sweetness and thickness to your liking. This smoothie offers a unique blend of flavors with the tartness of raspberries and the crunch of pistachios. Sip and savor the Raspberry Pistachio Pleasure!

Coconut Banana Cream

Ingredients

- 1 Banana
- 1/4 cup Coconut Cream
- 2 scoops Vanilla Protein Powder
- 1/2 cup Coconut Water

Instructions

1. Peel and slice the banana.

2. In a blender, combine banana slices, coconut cream, vanilla protein powder, and coconut water.

3. Blend the ingredients until you achieve a smooth and creamy texture.

4. If you prefer a colder smoothie, you can add a handful of ice cubes and blend again.

5. Taste the smoothie and adjust sweetness by adding more banana or a natural sweetener if desired.

6. Pour the Coconut Banana Cream into a glass, and optionally garnish with a sprinkle of shredded coconut.

7. Enjoy the tropical and creamy goodness of the Coconut Banana Cream smoothie!

Note

- Customize the sweetness and thickness according to your preferences. This smoothie offers a delightful combination of banana and coconut, providing a taste of the tropics with the added benefits of protein. Sip and savor the Coconut Banana Cream!

Maple Pecan Perfection

Ingredients

- 1/4 cup Pecans
- 2 tablespoons Maple Syrup
- 1/4 cup Oats
- 1 cup Whole Milk

Instructions

1. In a blender, combine the pecans, maple syrup, oats, and whole milk.

2. Blend the ingredients until you achieve a smooth and nutty texture.

3. If you prefer a thicker smoothie, you can add more oats gradually and blend again.

4. Taste the smoothie and adjust sweetness by adding more maple syrup if desired.

5. Pour the Maple Pecan Perfection into a glass, and optionally garnish with a sprinkle of chopped pecans on top.

6. Enjoy the rich and comforting flavors of maple and pecans in this delicious smoothie!

Note

- Customize the sweetness and thickness to suit your preferences. This smoothie provides a delightful blend of maple sweetness and the crunch of pecans, creating a comforting and satisfying drink. Sip and savor the Maple Pecan Perfection!

Chia Seed Pudding Paradise

Ingredients

- 2 tablespoons Chia Seeds
- 1 Banana
- 2 tablespoons Almond Butter
- 1 cup Almond Milk

Instructions

1. In a blender, combine chia seeds, sliced banana, almond butter, and almond milk.

2. Blend the ingredients until you achieve a smooth and puddinglike consistency.

3. Allow the mixture to sit for a few minutes to let the chia seeds absorb the liquid and thicken the smoothie.

4. If you prefer a colder smoothie, you can refrigerate the mixture for a while or add ice cubes before blending.

5. Taste the smoothie and adjust sweetness by adding more banana or a natural sweetener if desired.

6. Pour the Chia Seed Pudding Paradise into a glass, and optionally garnish with a banana slice or a sprinkle of chia seeds on top.

7. Enjoy the nutritious and satisfying Chia Seed Pudding Paradise!

Note

- Customize the sweetness and thickness according to your preferences. This smoothie combines the goodness of chia seeds, banana, and almond butter for a delightful and nutrient-rich treat. Sip and savor the Chia Seed Pudding Paradise!

Cinnamon Roll Heaven

Ingredients

- 1 Banana
- 1/2 teaspoon Cinnamon
- 1/4 cup Oats
- 2 scoops Vanilla Protein Powder
- 1 cup Whole Milk

Instructions

1. Peel and slice the banana.
2. In a blender, combine banana slices, cinnamon, oats, vanilla protein powder, and whole milk.
3. Blend the ingredients until you achieve a smooth and cinnamon-infused texture.
4. If you prefer a colder smoothie, you can add a handful of ice cubes and blend again.
5. Taste the smoothie and adjust sweetness or spiciness by adding more banana or cinnamon if desired.
6. Pour the Cinnamon Roll Heaven into a glass, and optionally sprinkle a dash of cinnamon on top for added flavor.
7. Enjoy the delicious and comforting taste of a cinnamon roll in liquid form!

Note

- Customize the sweetness and thickness according to your preferences. This smoothie provides the delightful flavors of a cinnamon roll while incorporating the nutritional benefits of oats and protein powder. Sip and savor the Cinnamon Roll Heaven!

Pineapple Cashew Crush

Ingredients

- 1 cup Pineapple chunks
- 1/4 cup Cashews
- 1/2 cup Coconut Milk
- 1/4 cup Greek Yogurt

Instructions

1. Prepare the pineapple by cutting it into chunks.

2. In a blender, combine the pineapple chunks, cashews, coconut milk, and Greek yogurt.

3. Blend the ingredients until you achieve a smooth and tropical-flavored consistency.

4. If you prefer a colder smoothie, you can add a handful of ice cubes and blend again.

5. Taste the smoothie and adjust sweetness or thickness by adding more pineapple or coconut milk if desired.

6. Pour the Pineapple Cashew Crush into a glass, and optionally garnish with a slice of pineapple for presentation.

7. Enjoy the refreshing and nutty goodness of the Pineapple Cashew Crush!

Note

- Customize the sweetness and thickness according to your preferences. This smoothie combines the tropical sweetness of pineapple with the creaminess of cashews and coconut milk, providing a delightful and nutritious beverage. Sip and savor the Pineapple Cashew Crush!

Fig and Walnut Fantasy

Ingredients

- 1 cup Figs (dried or fresh, stems removed)
- 1/4 cup Walnuts
- 1 tablespoon Honey
- 1 cup Almond Milk

Instructions

1. Using dried figs, soak them in warm water for a few minutes to soften.
2. In a blender, combine the figs, walnuts, honey, and almond milk.
3. Blend the ingredients until you achieve a smooth and nutty texture.
4. If you prefer a colder smoothie, you can add a handful of ice cubes and blend again.
5. Taste the smoothie and adjust sweetness by adding more honey if desired.
6. Pour the Fig and Walnut Fantasy into a glass, and optionally garnish with a whole walnut on top.
7. Enjoy the rich and indulgent flavors of figs and walnuts in this delightful smoothie!

Note

- Customize the sweetness and thickness according to your preferences. This smoothie captures the essence of an Almond Joy candy bar while incorporating the benefits of almond butter and protein powder. Sip and savor the Almond Joy Delight!

Almond Joy Delight

Ingredients

- 22 tablespoons Almond Butter
- 2 tablespoons Coconut Flakes
- 2 scoops Chocolate Protein Powder
- 1 cup Almond Milk

Instructions

1. In a blender, combine almond butter, coconut flakes, chocolate protein powder, and almond milk.

2. Blend the ingredients until you achieve a smooth and indulgent consistency.

3. If you prefer a colder smoothie, you can add a handful of ice cubes and blend again.

4. Taste the smoothie and adjust sweetness by adding more almond butter or a natural sweetener if desired.

5. Pour the Almond Joy Delight into a glass, and optionally sprinkle additional coconut flakes on top for extra flair.

6. Enjoy the delightful combination of almond, coconut, and chocolate flavors in this satisfying smoothie!

Note

- Customize the sweetness and thickness according to your preferences. This smoothie captures the essence of an Almond Joy candy bar while incorporating the benefits of almond butter and protein powder. Sip and savor the Almond Joy Delight!

Pumpkin Pie Powerhouse

Ingredients

- 1/2 cup Pumpkin Puree
- 1/4 cup Oats
- 1/2 teaspoon Cinnamon
- 2 scoops Vanilla Protein Powder
- 1 cup Whole Milk

Instructions

1. In a blender, combine pumpkin puree, oats, cinnamon, vanilla protein powder, and whole milk.

2. Blend the ingredients until you achieve a smooth and pumpkin pie-spiced texture.

3. If you prefer a colder smoothie, you can add a handful of ice cubes and blend again.

4. Taste the smoothie and adjust sweetness or spice by adding more pumpkin puree or cinnamon if desired.

5. Pour the Pumpkin Pie Powerhouse into a glass, and optionally sprinkle a dash of cinnamon on top for added flavor.

6. Enjoy the delicious and comforting taste of pumpkin pie in liquid form!

Note

- Customize the sweetness and thickness according to your preferences. This smoothie brings the warm and cozy flavors of pumpkin pie while incorporating the benefits of oats and protein powder. Sip and savor the Pumpkin Pie Powerhouse!

**Coffee Peanut Butter Craze

Ingredients

- 1/2 cup Pomegranate Seeds
- 1/4 cup Pecans
- 1/2 cup Greek Yogurt
- 1 cup Almond Milk

Instructions

1. In a blender, combine pomegranate seeds, pecans, Greek yogurt, and almond milk.

2. Blend the ingredients until you achieve a smooth and blissful consistency.

3. If you prefer a colder smoothie, you can add a handful of ice cubes and blend again.

4. Taste the smoothie and adjust sweetness or thickness by adding more pomegranate seeds or almond milk if desired.

5. Pour the Pomegranate Pecan Bliss into a glass, and optionally garnish with a few whole pecans for a delightful crunch.

6. Enjoy the refreshing and nutty goodness of the Pomegranate Pecan Bliss!

Note

- Customize the sweetness and thickness according to your preferences. This smoothie combines the vibrant taste of pomegranate with the nutty crunch of pecans, creating a blissful and nutritious beverage. Sip and savor the Pomegranate Pecan Bliss!

Pomegran- ate Pecan Bliss

Ingredients

- 1/2 cup Pomegranate Seeds
- 1/4 cup Pecans
- 1/2 cup Greek Yogurt
- 1 cup Almond Milk

Instructions

1. In a blender, combine pomegran- ate seeds, pecans, Greek yogurt, and almond milk.
2. Blend the ingredients until you achieve a smooth and blissful consistency.
3. If you prefer a colder smoothie, you can add a handful of ice cubes and blend again.
4. Taste the smoothie and adjust sweetness or thickness by add- ing more pomegranate seeds or almond milk if desired.
5. Pour the Pomegranate Pecan Bliss into a glass, and optionally gar- nish with a few whole pecans for a delightful crunch.
6. Enjoy the refreshing and nutty goodness of the Pomegranate Pecan Bliss!

Note

- Customize the sweetness and thick- ness according to your preferences. This smoothie combines the vibrant taste of pomegranate with the nutty crunch of pecans, creating a blissful and nutritious beverage. Sip and savor the Pomegranate Pecan Bliss!

Apricot Almond Ambrosia

Ingredients

- 1 cup Apricots (pitted and sliced)
- 1/4 cup Almonds
- 2 scoops Vanilla Protein Powder
- 1 cup Almond Milk

Instructions

1. Pit and slice the apricots.
2. In a blender, combine the sliced apricots, almonds, vanilla protein powder, and almond milk.
3. Blend the ingredients until you achieve a smooth and ambrosial texture.
4. If you prefer a colder smoothie, you can add a handful of ice cubes and blend again.
5. Taste the smoothie and adjust sweetness or thickness by adding more apricots or almond milk if desired.
6. Pour the Apricot Almond Ambrosia into a glass, and optionally garnish with a few sliced almonds for an extra touch.
7. Enjoy the delightful and refreshing flavors of apricots and almonds in this ambrosial smoothie!

Note

- Customize the sweetness and thickness according to your preferences. This smoothie combines the sweetness of apricots with the nutty goodness of almonds, creating a refreshing and protein-packed drink. Sip and savor the Apricot Almond Ambrosia!

Hazelnut Banana Cream

Ingredients

- 1/4 cup Hazelnuts
- 1 Banana
- 1/2 cup Greek Yogurt
- 1 tablespoon Honey
- 1 cup Almond Milk

Instructions

1. In a blender, combine hazelnuts, banana, Greek yogurt, honey, and almond milk.

2. Blend the ingredients until you achieve a smooth and creamy hazelnut banana cream texture.

3. If you prefer a colder smoothie, you can add a handful of ice cubes and blend again.

4. Taste the smoothie and adjust sweetness by adding more honey if desired.

5. Pour the Hazelnut Banana Cream into a glass, and optionally drizzle a bit of honey on top for extra sweetness.

6. Enjoy the rich and nutty flavors of hazelnuts combined with the creamy texture of banana and Greek yogurt!

Note

- Customize the sweetness and thickness according to your preferences. This smoothie provides a delightful blend of hazelnuts and banana, creating a creamy and satisfying beverage. Sip and savor the Hazelnut Banana Cream!

Cranberry Walnut Wonder

Ingredients

- 1/2 cup Cranberries (fresh or frozen)
- 1/4 cup Walnuts
- 2 scoops Vanilla Protein Powder
- 1 cup Almond Milk

Instructions

1. If using fresh cranberries, rinse them thoroughly.

2. In a blender, combine cranberries, walnuts, vanilla protein powder, and almond milk.

3. Blend the ingredients until you achieve a smooth and wonderous texture.

4. If you prefer a colder smoothie, you can add a handful of ice cubes and blend again.

5. Taste the smoothie and adjust sweetness or thickness by adding more cranberries or almond milk if desired.

6. Pour the Cranberry Walnut Wonder into a glass, and optionally garnish with a sprinkle of crushed walnuts on top.

7. Enjoy the tangy sweetness of cranberries combined with the crunch of walnuts in this wonderful smoothie!

Note

- Customize the sweetness and thickness according to your preferences. This smoothie provides a delightful blend of tart cranberries and the earthy richness of walnuts, creating a flavorful and nutritious beverage. Sip and savor the Cranberry Walnut Wonder!

Butter-scotch Ba-nana Bonanza

Ingredients

- 2 tablespoons Butterscotch Chips
- 1 Banana
- 1/4 cup Oats
- 1 cup Whole Milk

Instructions

1. In a blender, combine butterscotch chips, banana, oats, and whole milk.

2. Blend the ingredients until you achieve a smooth and bonanza-worthy texture.

3. If you prefer a colder smoothie, you can add a handful of ice cubes and blend again.

4. Taste the smoothie and adjust sweetness by adding more butterscotch chips or a natural sweetener if desired.

5. Pour the Butterscotch Banana Bonanza into a glass, and optionally top it with a few additional butterscotch chips for an extra treat.

6. Enjoy the delightful combination of butterscotch sweetness and banana goodness in this bonanza of flavors!

Note

- Customize the sweetness and thickness according to your preferences. This smoothie brings together the rich taste of butterscotch with the natural sweetness of banana, creating a bonanza for your taste buds. Sip and savor the Butterscotch Banana Bonanza!

Mango Pistachio Pleasure

Ingredients

- 1 cup Mango (diced)
- 1/4 cup Pistachios
- 1/2 cup Greek Yogurt
- 1/2 cup Coconut Water

Instructions

1. In a blender, combine diced mango, pistachios, Greek yogurt, and coconut water.

2. Blend the ingredients until you achieve a smooth and pleasurable consistency.

3. If you prefer a colder smoothie, you can add a handful of ice cubes and blend again.

4. Taste the smoothie and adjust sweetness or thickness by adding more mango or coconut water if desired.

5. Pour the Mango Pistachio Pleasure into a glass, and optionally garnish with a sprinkle of crushed pistachios on top.

6. Enjoy the tropical delight of mango combined with the nutty goodness of pistachios in this pleasurable smoothie!

Note

- Customize the sweetness and thickness according to your preferences. This smoothie offers a refreshing blend of mango and the crunch of pistachios, providing a pleasurable and nutrient-rich beverage. Sip and savor the Mango Pistachio Pleasure!

BOOK 2

How To

GAIN WEIGHT

On a Liquid Diet

RACHELLE K. SANDERS

Copyright

Disclaimer

Disclaimer: The images in this book are for illustrative purposes only and may not perfectly replicate the end product based on individual variations in ingredients, techniques, and personal interpretation. Results may differ, but we hope the flavors remain delightful on your culinary journey.

Table of Contents

Introduction

Reasons why someone might choose a liquid diet while also wanting to gain weight.

There are several reasons a person who wants to gain weight might choose to only drink his/her way through it. Even though it might seem odd, there are several reasons a person who wants to gain weight might choose a liquid diet. Here are some potential scenarios:

MEDICAL CONDITIONS

Digestive problems: People with gastroparesis, Crohn's disease, or bowel blockages may find it hard to digest solid food and need to stick to a liquid diet. But putting on weight might still be good for your health and healing.

Dental or oral injuries: After surgery or if you hurt your jaw, it may be painful or impossible to breathe or chew solid food, so you may need to stick to a liquid diet for a while. Putting on weight may be important for recovering from surgery and keeping your muscle strength.

Dysphagia, or trouble swallowing, is a neurological disease or a weakness in the muscles that can make it hard to swallow solid food. If nothing else works, a liquid diet might be the only choice. Making sure you gain weight is important to avoid starvation and health problems.

OTHER REASONS

Loss of appetite: Some people with medical conditions or who take certain medicines have a loss of appetite, which makes it hard to eat enough calories from solid foods. It may be easier for them to eat liquid foods, and they may help them get enough calories.

Convenience and portability: People who are busy or do not have easy access to solid foods may find that liquid diets make it easier to eat high-calorie meals and snacks on the go.

Dietary restrictions: Sometimes, someone with strict dietary needs may find it easier to meet their calorie and protein needs through carefully planned liquid meals.

It is important to remember that a liquid diet to gain weight should only be done carefully and with the help of a registered dietitian and a medical expert. They can help you make a plan that fits your needs, makes sure you get enough nutrition, and helps you gain weight in a healthy way.

Challenges of gaining weight, especially on a liquid diet:

GENERAL CHALLENGES

Appetite suppression: To gain weight, you need to consistently eat more calories than you burn. However, people who are having trouble gaining weight often do not want to eat enough and have trouble eating enough.

Nutrient deficiencies: Limiting the types of foods you eat can make you less likely to get enough protein, fiber, and some vitamins and minerals, which can make it harder to gain weight and be healthy overall.

Gaining muscle vs. fat: A lot of people have trouble gaining lean muscle mass and end up gaining more fat. Targeted protein intake and exercise are needed to build muscle, which can be harder to do when you are on a liquid diet.

Psychological factors: Problems with body image, upset eating, and eating disorders can make it hard to gain weight.

CHALLENGES SPECIFIC TO A LIQUID DIET

Satiety and fullness: liquids do not make you feel full like solid foods do, which makes it harder to reach and keep a calorie excess.

Fiber deficiency: Most liquid diets do not have enough fiber, which can cause stomach problems like constipation and hurt the health of your gut.

Limited food variety: liquid diets can get boring, and people can get tired of the tastes, which makes them eat even fewer calories.

Planning and preparation: Making liquid meals that are high in calories and nutrients can take more time and need more planning than normal meals.

Social limitations: Eating and socializing go hand in hand, and liquid diets can make it hard to join in on sharing meals and social events.

These are some of the problems people have when they are trying to gain weight, especially when they are only drinking water. Remember that talking to a doctor and a registered dietitian is very important for making a safe, successful, and personalized plan to gain weight.

How important it is to talk to a doctor or other health practitioners before starting any diet plan.

It is important to talk to a doctor before starting a liquid diet plan to gain weight for a number of reasons:

HEALTH AND SAFETY

Undiagnosed medical conditions: Some health conditions can make a liquid diet harmful or change how to gain weight properly. A medical worker can access your health and tell you about any problems that might be happening.

Nutrient deficiencies: It is easy to lose track of important nutrients when you only eat liquids. A registered dietitian can help you make a custom plan to make sure you get all the nutrients you need to gain weight in a healthy way.

Medication interactions: Some medicines may not work as well when you change what you eat, or they may mix with other medicines you take. A registered dietitian can make sure that your food plan does not conflict with the medicines you are taking.

Digestive problems: If you do not plan and keep an eye on your liquid diet, it can make digestive problems worse. A medical worker can find any underlying issues and suggest the best ways to fix them.

EFFECTIVENESS AND SUSTAINABILITY

Setting reasonable weight gain goals and making a plan that fits your needs and body type is something that a healthcare worker can help you do.

Muscle gain vs. fat gain: Increasing lean muscle mass takes more than just eating more calories. A registered dietitian can help you figure out how to combine exercise and protein diet to help you build muscle.

Long-term success: A healthcare worker can help you form healthy habits and behaviors that will help you gain and keep off the weight. This will prevent you from yo-yo dieting and gaining the weight back.

EMOTIONAL AND PSYCHOLOGICAL SUPPORT

Dealing with the root causes: Having trouble gaining weight can be caused by mental or emotional issues. A medical worker can find any underlying problems and help you find the right help if you need it.

Accountability and inspiration: Talking to a doctor or nurse can give you ongoing support and motivation, which can help you stick to your weight gain goals.

As always, your health and happiness are the most important things. Before starting any diet plan, but especially one as specialized as a liquid diet for weight gain, you should talk to a doctor, nurse or a registered dietitian/nutritionist. This will make sure that you reach your goals safely, effectively, and with the best chance of success.

Chapter 1:

The Basics

THE GENERAL RULES OF CALORIE INTAKE AND EXPENDITURE.

An understanding of the general rules of calorie intake and expenditure can be gained from the idea of energy balance:

ENERGY INTAKE:

Calories is the measure how much energy food and drinks give us.
Food and drink are how we "take in" energy.
There are different amounts of calories in different foods and drinks.

ENERGY EXPENDITURE:

Our bodies need energy for the execution of its functions, such as:
Basal Metabolic Rate (BMR), which is the amount of energy our bodies need to do basic things like breathing, heartbeat, and organ activity. Age, sex, and body type are some of the things that affect BMR.
Physical Activity: Moving around every day and working out use up some energy.
The energy needed to break down and absorb food is called the thermic effect of food (TEF).

BALANCE OF ENERGY:

When we take in the same amount of energy as we use, our weight stays the same.

When we take in more energy than we use, our bodies store the extra energy as fat or muscle, which makes us gain weight.

When we burn more calories than we take in, our bodies use saved energy (like fat or muscle) to make up for the deficit.

The following points are worth remembering:

Different people have different calorie needs based on their age, gender, body size, level of exercise, and metabolism.

To maintain a healthy weight, you need to know how many calories you need and make sure you do not take in more than you burn.

Keeping track of the calories you eat and burn can help you control your weight and reach your goals.

This book is mostly about weight gain, but understanding energy balance helps people stay at a healthy weight after they hit their goal.

The importance of different macronutrients (protein, carbohydrates, and fats) for healthy weight gain.

Each macronutrient is important for good weight gain in its own way, helping with different parts of the process:

PROTEIN:

For growing muscle, you need protein. Protein is what muscles are made of. Protein intake of 0.8 to 1 gram per pound of body weight is necessary to promote muscle growth and development, especially when strength training is added to the mix.

Satiety: Protein can make you feel fuller for longer, which can help you control your hunger and keep you from eating too much.

Metabolic rate: Protein takes more energy to digest and process than other macronutrients. This means that eating protein slightly speeds up your metabolism and makes you burn more calories.

SUGARS AND CARBS:

Energy source: Carbohydrates are the best way for the body to get fast energy for daily tasks and exercise. Complex carbohydrates from whole grains, fruits, and veggies give you long-lasting energy that you can use to build muscle and power through workouts.

Glycogen storage: Carbohydrates are kept in the liver and muscles as glycogen, which can be used right away for energy needs during activity.

Fiber: You can get fiber from fruits, veggies, and whole grains. Fiber is good for your digestive health and can help your body absorb nutrients.

FATS:

Calorie density: Fats have more calories per gram than protein and carbs. This means it is easier to reach your weight gain goals of eating more calories than you burn.

Hormone balance: Nuts, bananas, and fatty fish are all good sources of healthy fats that help your body make healthy hormones, like testosterone, which can help your muscles grow.

Satiety: Healthy fats can help you feel full and satisfied, which can help you control your hunger and cravings.

Nutrients' usage: Some vitamins, like A, D, E, and K, are fat-soluble, which means they need fat to be absorbed properly.

THE KEY IS BALANCE:

Each macronutrient is important, but to gain weight in a healthy way, you need to find the right balance for your individual needs and goals. These ratios might need to be changed depending on how active you are, what your body looks like, and your unique goals.

Talking to a trained dietitian can help you make a personalized macronutrient plan that will help you gain weight and improve your health and well-being as a whole.

Specific challenges of gaining muscle mass on a liquid diet.

Getting bigger muscles is harder when you are on a liquid diet instead of a solid food plan. Here are some important things to think about:

PROTEIN INTAKE

Lower protein density: Many snacks and meals that you drink may naturally have less protein than whole foods like meat, chicken, and fish.

Problems with meeting high-protein needs: It can be hard to drink a lot of protein because it can make you feel full or tired of the taste of it quickly.

Incomplete protein sources: Some liquid protein sources, like plant-based milks, may not have all the necessary amino acids that your muscles need to grow.

BREAKING DOWN AND ABSORBING

Protein processing is slower: liquids digest faster than solids, which could make it harder for your body to keep releasing proteins over time, which is important for muscle growth.

Less eating and feeling full: eating solid food releases hormones in the gut that make you feel full and help digestion. These processes can be slowed down if you do not chew as with drinks.

Fiber deficiency: Most liquid diets do not have enough fiber, which can hurt gut health and make it harder to absorb nutrients like protein.

TAKE THESE THINGS INTO ACCOUNT:

Limited food variety: If you only eat liquid meals, it can be hard to get enough energy before your workout and protein after your workout to fix your muscles.

Balance of electrolytes and water: Liquid diets can make it easy to forget about balance of electrolytes and water, which is important for good exercise performance and recovery.

Mental factors: Sticking to a boring liquid diet may make you less motivated and less likely to stick to your plans, which could make you less likely to stick to your exercise habits.

SOME MORE PROBLEMS

Cost and preparation: Making liquid meals that are high in protein and calories can take a lot of time and planning, which could make them more expensive than solid food choices.

Social limits: Eating and talking to other people often go hand in hand. If you are on a liquid diet, it might be hard to eat out or go to social events.

Digestive problems: Someone who only feed on liquids might have digestive problems or constipation because they do not get enough fiber or chewing activity.

GETTING PAST THESE PROBLEMS

Focus on drinks that are high in protein. In your liquid meals, include protein-rich foods like protein powders, Greek yogurt, nut butters, and blended lean meats.

Plan ahead and try new things. Pick meals that use a variety of protein sources and mix them with high-calorie foods like healthy fats and complex carbohydrates.

You might want to take supplements. Protein powders and full amino acid supplements can help you get enough protein, especially if you are a vegan or vegetarian.

Put exercise first. Make sure you eat right before and after a workout by changing your meals to be more liquid or planning solid food snacks.

Talk to a doctor and a certified dietitian. They can make your diet plan unique, take into account your needs, and suggest ways to deal with these problems.

Remember that you can build muscle strength while on a liquid diet, but you need to plan carefully, pay attention to details, and deal with the unique challenges that come up. It is very important to talk to a doctor and a registered dietitian to make sure you reach your goals safely and efficiently.

Chapter 2:

Practical Considerations:

Take care of any stomach problems that might come up on a liquid diet.

If you stick to a liquid diet for a long time, it can cause a number of stomach problems, including:

CONSTIPATION

Lack of fiber: Liquid diets are typically low in fiber, which is needed to keep the gut moving and avoid constipation.

Lower gut transit time: liquids move through the digestive system faster than solid foods. This means that fiber does not have as much time to bulk up stools and make you go to the bathroom.

LEAKY GUT

Big changes to your diet: Making big changes to your diet can briefly upset your gut microbiome, which can cause diarrhea.

Artificial sweeteners: Some people get diarrhea from some artificial sweeteners that are used in commercial shakes and drinks.

Food sensitivities or intolerances: Diarrhea can be caused by sensitivities or intolerances to lactose or fructose in juices or dairy-based products.

GASTROESOPHAGEAL REFLUX DISEASE (GERD)

Drinking lots of liquid: Drinking a lot of liquid can make GERD symptoms worse by putting pressure on the lower esophageal wall. Certain foods and drinks: People with GERD can get heartburn and acid reflux from acidic fruits, fizzy drinks, and coffee.

BLOATING AND GAS

Air swallowing: This can happen when you drink quickly or with a straw, and it can make you bloat and have gas.
Fermentation: If your gut bacteria get used to a liquid diet high in sugar, it can cause more fermentation, which can cause gas and bloating.

ADDITIONAL COMPLICATIONS

Malnutrition: People who follow liquid diets for a long time may not get enough fiber, vitamins, and minerals, which can make their gut health and digestion even worse.
Unbalanced electrolytes: Drinking too much water without paying attention to your electrolytes can cause imbalances that can affect your digestion and other body processes.

MINIMIZING DIGESTIVE ISSUES

Introduce fiber slowly: Add leafy greens, chia seeds, or ground flaxseed, which are high in fiber, to your drinks one at a time.
Stay hydrated: Drink a lot of water throughout the day, but do not drink too much all at once.
Pick carefully: Pick liquids that are low in sugar and acid, and if you already have sensitivities, get rid of items that bother you.
Eating solid food as much as possible: To keep your gut healthy, eat small meals or snacks of solid food often.
To deal with GERD, stay away from things that make it worse, sleep with your head raised, and think about taking medicine if you need to. Talk to a doctor, nurse or certified dietitian about your digestive problems and get personalized tips on how to deal with them on a

liquid diet.

Remember how important it is to pay attention to your body and notice any stomach issues. If your symptoms do not go away or get worse, you should see a doctor to rule out any underlying problems and then make changes to your food.

Tips for managing hunger and cravings while drinking your meals.

On a liquid diet, hunger pangs and cravings can really get in the way of your weight gain goals. Here are some tips on how to handle them well:

FOCUS ON THINGS THAT MAKE YOU FEEL FULL

Protein: Make sure your liquid meals have high-protein foods like protein powder, Greek yogurt, nut butters, or mixed lean meats. Protein fills you up quickly and keeps you full for a long time.

Healthy fats: To your liquid meals, add healthy fats like avocado, nut butter, seeds, or high-fat dairy items. These fats make you feel full and slow down processing.

Fiber: Adding chia seeds, ground flaxseed, or blended green veggies to liquids can be hard, but they can help add fiber. Fiber helps your body digest food and makes you feel full.

INCLUDE TECHNIQUES FOR EATING WITH AWARENESS

Slow down and enjoy each sip. This gives your body time to tell you it is full and keeps you from eating too much.

When you can, eat solid food snacks. Adding small, fiber-rich solid food snacks to your diet can help you feel fuller and control your cravings.

Stay refreshed. Being thirsty is often mistaken for being hungry. Getting a lot of water throughout the day can help cut down on fake hunger pangs. Whenever you feel hunger, take a cup of water first. The hunger might disappear if it is fake. If it persists, you could then go ahead to satisfy your hunger.

If you feel like giving in to a craving, do something else, like going for a walk, listening to music, or calling a friend, to take your mind off of it until the desire passes.

PLAN AND CHANGE THE LIQUID MEALS YOU EAT

Measure your amounts and keep track of the calories you eat to make sure you are eating enough to satisfy your body's requirement.

Calories per volume: Pick ingredients that are higher in calories and focus on liquids that are denser, like smoothies with nut butter or soups that have been blended, instead of low-calorie choices.

Variety is important. To avoid getting bored, try out new tastes, textures, and foods to keep your cravings at bay.

Take supplements. Fiber supplements or glutamine powder can help you feel fuller and control your cravings even more.

Some more tips:

Pay attention to your body; stop drinking when you are full, not stuffed. Ignoring signs that you are full can make you eat too much and feel uncomfortable.

Deal with your worry. worry can make you hungry and cause cravings. To deal with worry, try deep breathing, yoga, meditation, or other ways to relax.

Get help: If you are on a liquid diet, talk to your doctor or a registered dietitian for personalized tips and help with dealing with hunger and cravings.

Remember that there are more than one way to deal with hunger and cravings while on a liquid diet. You can get through this struggle and reach your weight gain goals if you follow these tips and are patient and dedicated.

How to stay hydrated and keep the balance of electrolytes.

It is very important for your health to stay hydrated and keep your chemical balance, and it is even more important if you are on a liquid diet. Here are some important tips:

STAYING HYDRATED

Keep an eye on your pee. It should be clear or pale yellow at most. Darker pee means you are dehydrated.

Set reminders: If drinking water is the only way you stay hydrated, remind yourself to drink throughout the day, even if you do not feel thirsty.

Track how much water you drink. Apps or water bottles with markings can help you monitor your water intake and ensure you meet your daily needs.

Pick your liquids carefully. Water is important, but you should also drink herbal teas, coconut water, and diluted fruit juices to add variety and nutrients.

Avoid drinks that make you thirsty. Limit coffee, sugary drinks, and alcohol because they can make you pee a lot and make you thirstier.

BALANCE OF ELECTROLYTES:

Focus on foods that are high in electrolytes. Even if you are only drinking water, include fresh greens, nuts, seeds, avocados, and fruits that are high in potassium, like bananas and oranges.

Think about taking electrolyte supplements. Powders or tablets that contain electrolytes can help, especially if you sweat a lot or work out often. Pick a vitamin that is well-balanced, and talk to your doctor before taking any.

Keep an eye out for signs of imbalance, such as headaches, tiredness, muscle cramps, feeling dizzy, or feeling sick. If you have these signs, you should talk to a doctor or nurse.

Pay attention to your body; thirst is not the only sign that you are thirsty. If you are tired, smell funny, or have headaches, it could mean that your electrolytes are out of balance.

SOME MORE TIPS

Talk to your doctor, nurse or registered dietitian. They can give you personalized advice on how to stay hydrated and balance your electrolytes based on your needs and health.

Keep an eye on how active you are. Being active and hot weather, both make you need more fluids and electrolytes. Adapt your water intake as required.

Do not drink too much water: Some people drink too much water, but it can also be bad for you. Follow the rules given and keep an eye on your electrolyte levels.

Watch out for medicines: some medicines can change the balance of electrolytes. If you are taking any Know that staying hydrated and keeping your electrolyte balance is important for your health, weight gain, and the way your body works. You can make sure that your liquid diet meets your needs and supports your health by using these tips and talking to a medical professional.

Tips on how to spread out your meals and snacks during the day.

It is important to space out your meals and snacks if you want to control your hunger, feel full, and stick to your calorie goals while on a liquid diet. Take a look at these strategies:

HOW OFTEN

Aim for smaller meals more often. Instead of three big meals, try five or six smaller snacks or liquid meals every two to three hours. This helps keep your energy level steady and keeps you from eating too much later.

Do not be too strict with your plan; listen to your body. You should eat when you are hungry and stop when you are full.

Plan your day: Make a list of your liquid meals and snacks ahead of time so you do not have to make last-minute choices that might not be healthy or high in calories.

MEASURE OUT PORTIONS:

Make sure you do not eat too few calories by using measuring cups or containers to make sure you eat the right amount.

Start small and add slowly: Start with smaller amounts and add more slowly as you get used to the new routine and watch how hungry you are.

Pay attention to nutrient density. To get the most calories and nutrients in each serving, choose foods like protein powders, nut butters, healthy fats, and leafy veggies.

EAT WITH AWARENESS

Slow down and enjoy: Drink slowly and chew on ice chips or frozen fruit if you are drinking milkshakes. When you eat more slowly, your body has more time to tell you when it is full, which keeps you from eating too much.

Use your senses: Pay attention to how your liquid foods taste, feel, and temperature. This can make things more fun and satisfying.

Keep your distractions to a minimum by not writing, watching TV, or using your phone while you eat. Being distracted can make you buy things without thinking and ignore signs that you are full.

Some more tips:

Include solid snacks: Eat small amounts of solid food between liquid meals to get more fiber and texture, which will help control your hunger and wants even more.

Plan liquid meals before you work out. Carbohydrate and protein-rich pre-workout liquid meals give you energy and help your muscles heal. Change what you eat after working out: for best muscle repair and growth, eat protein-rich liquid meals or snacks right after your workout.

Get help from a registered dietitian. They can help you make a meal plan and pacing plan that fits your wants and goals.

Do not forget that it takes practice to find the best way to time your meals and snacks for your body and plan. To best gain weight and support good eating habits that last, be open to change, try new things, and pay attention to your body's signals.

How to incorporate exercise into your weight gain plan

Even if you are only drinking your meals, exercise is an important part of a good weight gain plan. Here are some good ways to include it:

TYPES OF WORK OUT

Strength training: This is the most important thing you can do to build strength. Focus on workouts like squats, deadlifts, rows, and presses that work more than one muscle group at once. To help your muscles get bigger, use moderate weights and do a lot of reps (8–12). Aim to do 30 to 60 minutes of moderate-intensity exercise most days of the week. This could be brisk walking, swimming, or cycling. This helps you get in better shape overall and is good for your heart.

HIIT (High-Intensity Interval Training): Doing short bursts of high-intensity exercise followed by rest periods can also be helpful, but if you have any health issues, talk to your doctor before you start.

CONSIDERATIONS FOR LIQUID DIET

Pre-workout nutrition: About 30 to 60 minutes before you work out, eat a liquid food that is high in carbs and protein. This will give you energy and keep your muscles from breaking down.

Post-workout fuel: To help your muscles grow and heal, eat or drink something protein-rich right away after working out.

Hydration: Drink plenty of water all day, but especially before, during, and after working out.

Balance of electrolytes: If you sweat a lot or work out hard, you might want to take electrolyte supplements to avoid imbalances.

Pay attention to your body: Begin with a lower level of effort and slowly add more time and intensity as your fitness level rises. When you first start working out, do not push yourself too hard.

SOME MORE TIPS

Work with a teacher: If you want to reach your fitness goals safely and effectively, you should think about hiring a certified personal trainer. Talk to a medical practitioner or certified dietician about your exercise plans. This is especially important if you have any health problems or have not worked out in a while.

Find activities you enjoy: Exercising should be enjoyable, not a chore. Choose activities you find fun and engaging to increase your adherence to your workout routine.

Rest and healing should be your top priority. Give your body enough time to rest and recover between workouts. This is how long muscles need to heal and grow.

Stay motivated: To stay motivated, do things like set SMART goals, keep track of your progress, join a gym or a workout group, or give yourself rewards when you meet important goals.

Keep in mind that planning ahead, listening to your body, and making small steps are all important parts of adding exercise to your liquid diet weight gain plan.

By using these tips and getting help from a professional, you can safely and successfully gain muscle mass, improve your health, and reach your weight gain goals.

Chapter 3:

Success in the Long Run:

The important of building sustainable habits for healthy weight gain. It might be tempting to go on a crash diet to gain weight quickly, but the best way to gain and keep off the weight in the long term is to form healthy habits. Here is why:

PROS OF LONG-LASTING HABITS

Long-term success: Extreme diets or fad diets often do not work and cause people to go on and off diets, which hurts their long-term goals. You can stay healthy and lose weight if you focus on habits that you can keep up.

Better health: Long-term habits like eating well and exercising regularly improve health and well-being by lowering the risk of chronic diseases, giving you more energy, and making your mental health better.

Flexibility and enjoyment: long-lasting habits let you enjoy small treats and the social aspects of eating without feeling guilty or afraid of going off track. You can still eat well and reach your goals.

Integrating healthy habits into your daily life can help you gain weight and stay healthy. This way, you will not feel like you are constantly struggling or forced to forego things.

CREATING HABITS THAT LAST

Changes should be small at first. Change your diet and exercise routine little by little. Small changes that are easy to make are easier to stick with than big changes that are hard to do.

Enjoy it: Both eating and working out should be fun. Find healthy foods that you really enjoy and activities that you enjoy doing.

Planning and preparing: Making workout plans, meal plans, and healthy snack foods ahead of time can help you stay on track and avoid making bad choices when you are hungry or short on time.

Support system: Ask friends, family, or a registered dietitian to help you. Knowing that other people are behind you can help you stay motivated and responsible.

Mindfulness: When you eat and work out, be aware of what you are doing. Listen to your body when it tells you it is hungry or full, and be present during your workouts to get the most out of them and keep yourself motivated.

Set reasonable goals: Do not expect to gain weight overnight or set goals that are too high. A healthy weight gain rate is between 0.5 and 1 pound per week. Along the way, celebrate smaller wins.

Allow yourself to be forgiven; everyone has bad days. Don't let occasional slip-ups derail your progress. Acknowledge them, learn from them, and get back on track with self-compassion.

Sustainable weight gain is not about quick fixes or drastic measures. It's about building healthy habits you can enjoy and maintain for life. By prioritizing your overall well-being, practicing self-care, and focusing on long-term progress, you can achieve your weight gain goals without jeopardizing your health or happiness.

Tips for transitioning back to a solid food diet.

Successfully transitioning back to solid food after a liquid diet requires careful planning and mindful execution. Here are some tips to ensure a smooth and healthy shift:

GRADUAL REINTRODUCTION

Start slow: Begin by incorporating soft, easy-to-digest solid foods like mashed potatoes, yogurt, scrambled eggs, and cooked vegetables.
Increase complexity gradually: Slowly add more texture and fiber to your diet with cooked fruits, soft whole grains, and lean meats.
Listen to your body: Pay attention to any digestive discomfort and adjust your pace accordingly. Don't rush the process.

NUTRITION CONSIDERATIONS

Continue mindful eating: Maintain the healthy eating habits you established during your liquid diet, focusing on nutrient-dense foods and balanced meals.
Don't overeat: Solid food is more calorie-dense than liquids. Be mindful of portion sizes and avoid overeating, especially in the initial stages.
Hydrate adequately: Continue drinking plenty of water throughout the day to aid digestion and prevent constipation.
Some more tips:
Chew thoroughly: Slower eating and proper chewing allow your digestive system to adapt to solid food and absorb nutrients effectively.
Manage stress: Stress can disrupt digestion. Practice relaxation techniques like deep breathing or meditation to manage stress levels.
Seek professional guidance: Consult a registered dietitian or your healthcare professional for personalized advice and support during the transition.
Be patient: Remember, your body needs time to adjust. Allow yourself several weeks to fully transition back to solid food while monitoring

your progress and making adjustments as needed.

Below are some specific dietary considerations for different post-liquid diet phases:

FIRST WEEK:

Focus on soft, easily digestible foods.
Reintroduce fiber gradually to avoid constipation.
Continue liquid meals once or twice a day if needed.

SECOND WEEK:

Expand your food variety with cooked fruits, whole grains, and lean meats.
Increase fiber intake gradually.
Consider transitioning to three solid meals and one liquid meal per day.

THIRD WEEK AND BEYOND:

Aim for a balanced diet with all food groups covered.
Maintain healthy portion amounts and mindful eating habits.
Focus on long-term sustainable methods for healthy weight management.
Remember, transitioning back to solid food is a journey, not a goal. Be patient, listen to your body, and focus on building healthy, sustainable habits for long-term weight management and general well-being.

Address potential psychological challenges and offer strategies for keeping motivation.
Transitioning to or maintaining a liquid diet for weight gain can come with a host of psychological difficulties. Here are some possible hurdles and strategies to help you stay motivated:

CHALLENGES

Body image concerns: Focusing entirely on the scale or external factors might lead to dissatisfaction and frustration, especially in the beginning. Remember, weight gain needs time and a focus on good habits, not just the number on the scale.

Social limitations: Liquid diets can make it difficult to join in social events and meals, leading to feelings of isolation or missing out. Try finding alternative ways to socialize without compromising your diet, or explore meal choices you can enjoy with others.

Taste fatigue: Liquid meals can become monotonous, leading to cravings and wish for solid food. Experiment with different tastes, textures, and ingredients to keep your meals interesting.

Emotional eating: Underlying emotional issues might cause cravings or unhealthy eating habits. Seek help from a therapist or counselor to address these issues and build healthy coping mechanisms.

Motivation can fade when things do not go as planned or when you have problems. Enjoy small wins, keep track of your progress in good ways, and keep in mind your long-term goals and the reason you started this trip.

WAYS TO GET MOTIVATED

Set goals that you can actually reach. Do not just focus on the number on the scale; also, try to improve your health in general.

Visualize success: Write down your goals and how they will improve your life on a vision board or in a book.

Find people who can help you. Talk about your trip with family, friends, or online groups that are all about weight gain or liquid diets. Their support can be very helpful.

Celebrate big steps and accomplishments with prizes that are not food, like doing things you enjoy.

Self-compassion means being kind to yourself when you mess up. See them as chances to learn, not as mistakes.

Take a moment to enjoy the process of making good choices and taking care of your body. Accept the good changes that have happened to your energy, confidence, and health as a whole.

Keep in mind that losing or gaining weight is a personal process that will have ups and downs. You can find the drive and strength to stay on track, reach your goals, and have a better relationship with food and your body by dealing with the psychological issues and using these strategies.

Examples of meal plans for people with a range of calorie needs and goals

Note: These are just examples. For personalized meal plans that are tailored to your needs and health conditions, you should always talk to a registered dietitian or other health care worker.

1. 1800-CALORIE MEAL PLAN TO GET STRONGER

For breakfast:
Berry puree mixed with two scoops of protein powder
Avocado on two pieces of whole-wheat toast
Grass-topped Greek yogurt with fruit
A snack:
Cottage cheese with fruit and honey on top
A handful of different nuts and seeds
For lunch:
Fruits and veggies in a tuna salad with whole-wheat crackers
Whole-grain bread and black bean soup with a salad
A snack:
Smoothie with peanut butter, banana, and spinach
Cheese on apple slices
Food for dinner
Chicken breast on the grill with veggies and roasted sweet potato
A bowl of quinoa with roasted veggies, chickpeas, and tahini dressing
A snack:
Peanut butter and dark chocolate chips in Greek yogurt

2. 2500 CALORIE MEAL PLAN TO PUT ON WEIGHT

For breakfast:
Eggs cooked in spinach and cheese
Two pieces of whole-wheat toast with avocado spread on them
Oatmeal with nuts and berries

A snack:

Putting almond butter on a banana

Popcorn and string cheese

For lunch:

Salmon with steamed veggies and brown rice

Soup with lentils and whole-grain bread

Gluten-free burger on a whole-grain bun with sweet potato fries

A snack:

A fruit and protein bar

Nuts and dried fruit in a trail mix

Food for dinner

Stir-fried beef with brown rice and greens

Whole-wheat crust for chicken pot pie

Turkey ground up and mixed with pasta, marinara sauce, and veggies.

A snack:

Cottage cheese with fruit and coconut flakes on top

3. 1500-CALORIE MEAL PLAN TO KEEP YOUR WEIGHT AT A HEALTHY LEVEL

For breakfast:

Granola and berries on top of Greek yogurt

Cream cheese, smoked salmon, and whole-wheat bread

A smoothie made of almond milk, spinach, and banana

A snack:

The edamame

Ham and carrot sticks with hummus

For lunch:

Chicken or tofu on the grill, avocado, and balsamic sauce on a salad.

Whole-wheat tortilla wrap with turkey and vegetables

Lentil soup with a salad on the side

A snack:

Peanut butter on apple slices

Eggs that are hard-boiled

Food for dinner

Salmon baked in a pan with roasted veggies

Soy sauce, brown rice, and chicken stir-fry

Sweet potato fries and black bean burgers on whole-wheat buns.

A snack:

Greek yogurt with protein powder and different kinds of fruit

TIPS

You are welcome to change these meal plans to fit your tastes and food needs.

At every meal and snack, make sure you get protein, healthy fats, and complex carbs.

During the day, drink a lot of water.

Pay attention to your body and change how many calories you eat as needed.

To help you stay on track, you might want to use an app that counts calories.

Conclusion

In conclusion, building muscle mass on a liquid diet presents unique challenges, from protein intake hurdles and digestive issues to psychological hurdles and maintaining motivation. However, with careful planning, mindful execution, and addressing these challenges effectively, it is possible to achieve your goals.

Key points to remember:

Protein intake: Focus on high-protein liquids, consider supplements, and plan pre- and post-workout meals.
Digestive issues: Manage fiber intake, hydration, and potential sensitivities. Consult your doctor if symptoms persist.
Hunger and cravings: Prioritize satiety-promoting ingredients, practice mindful eating, and integrate solid food snacks when possible.
Hydration and electrolytes: Stay hydrated, consider electrolyte supplements, and monitor your body's response.
Pacing meals and snacks: Smaller, more frequent meals with portion control and nutrient density are key.
Exercise: Include strength training, moderate-intensity cardio, and work with a trainer if needed. Prioritize rest and recovery.
Sustainable habits: Focus on gradual changes, find enjoyment, and prioritize overall health and well-being.
Transition back to solid food: Start slowly, reintroduce fiber gradually, and listen to your body's cues. Seek professional guidance if needed.
Psychological challenges: Address body image concerns, social limitations, taste fatigue, and motivation decline with self-compassion, support networks, and goal visualization.

Sample meal plans: Consider different calorie needs and goals when creating your own personalized plans.

Troubleshooting common problems: Be prepared for digestive issues, nutrient deficiencies, taste fatigue, social limitations, and other challenges. Consult a healthcare professional or registered dietitian for personalized solutions.

Building muscle mass on a liquid diet requires dedication, adaptability, and addressing specific challenges. By following these tips and insights, you can navigate this journey safely and effectively, achieving your goals while developing healthy and sustainable habits for your well-being.

To your success

If you enjoyed the content of this book, take a moment to leave a feedback by submitting a review on Amazon. This will be the best way to show your support. Scan the QR code below to access the review page.

As a sign of my gratitude, I'm offering you an extra chapter on the subject of this book with the title "How to fix common issues that come up on a liquid diet". This will help you navigate the most prevalent challenges in the case they spring up in your journey. Scan to download

Books in this series:

1. <u>High Calorie Recipes for Weight Gain</u>

2. <u>STICK to THICK: A Complete Weight</u>

<u>Gain Plan for Underweight Women</u>

Other books by author:

Rachelle K. Sanders' <u>Book Collection</u>

Made in the USA
Monee, IL
14 October 2024